I0789132

Replicate the Drawing

With a dedication to nature lovers

SHARE YOUR DRAWINGS

ADVANCED LEVEL

Galas Products

There are some 320,000 species of plants, found on all continents, even Antarctica. Since more are discovered every year, that number will increase over time.

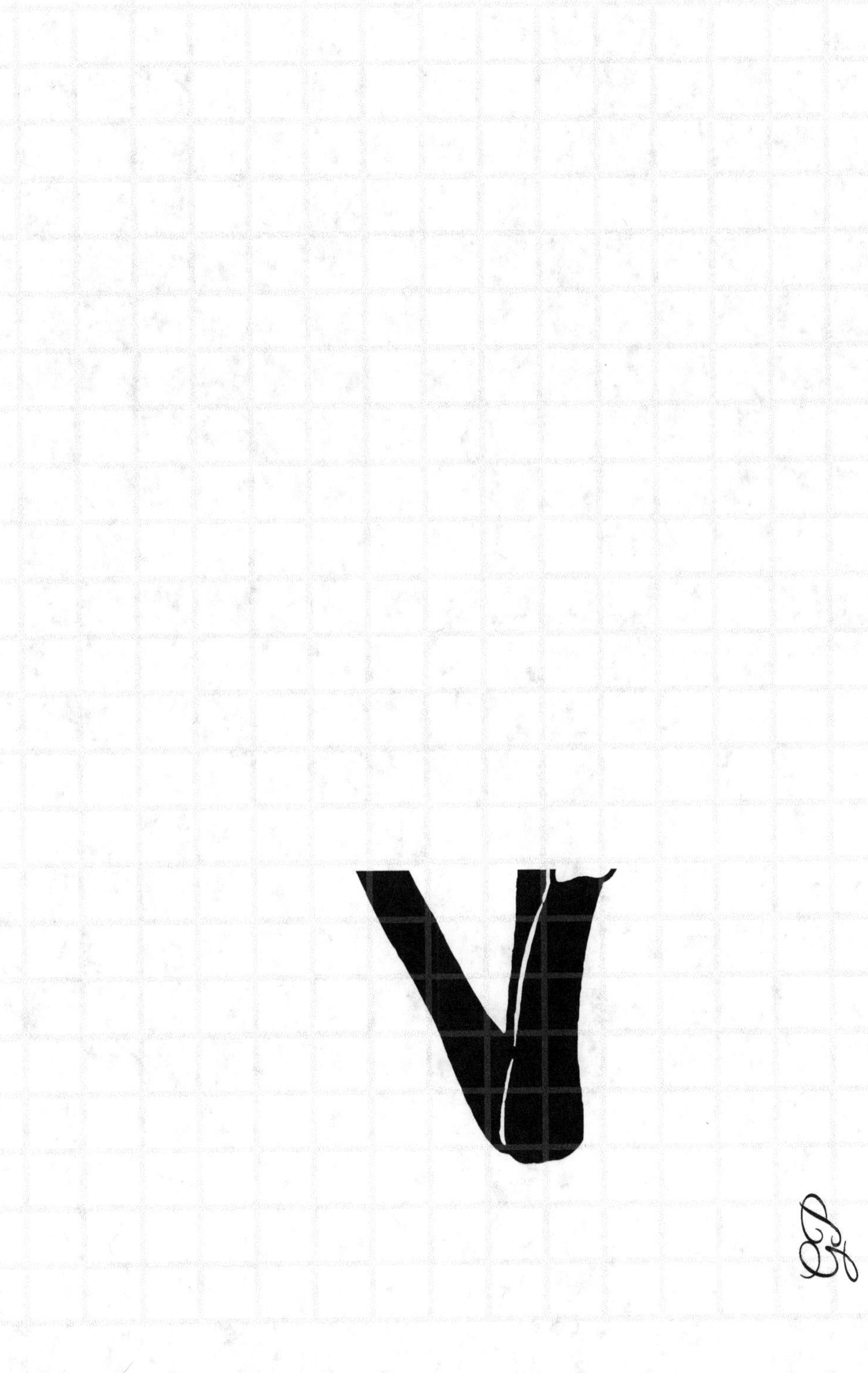

A single Portabella mushroom can contain more potassium than a banana.

Mushrooms are made up of around 90% water.

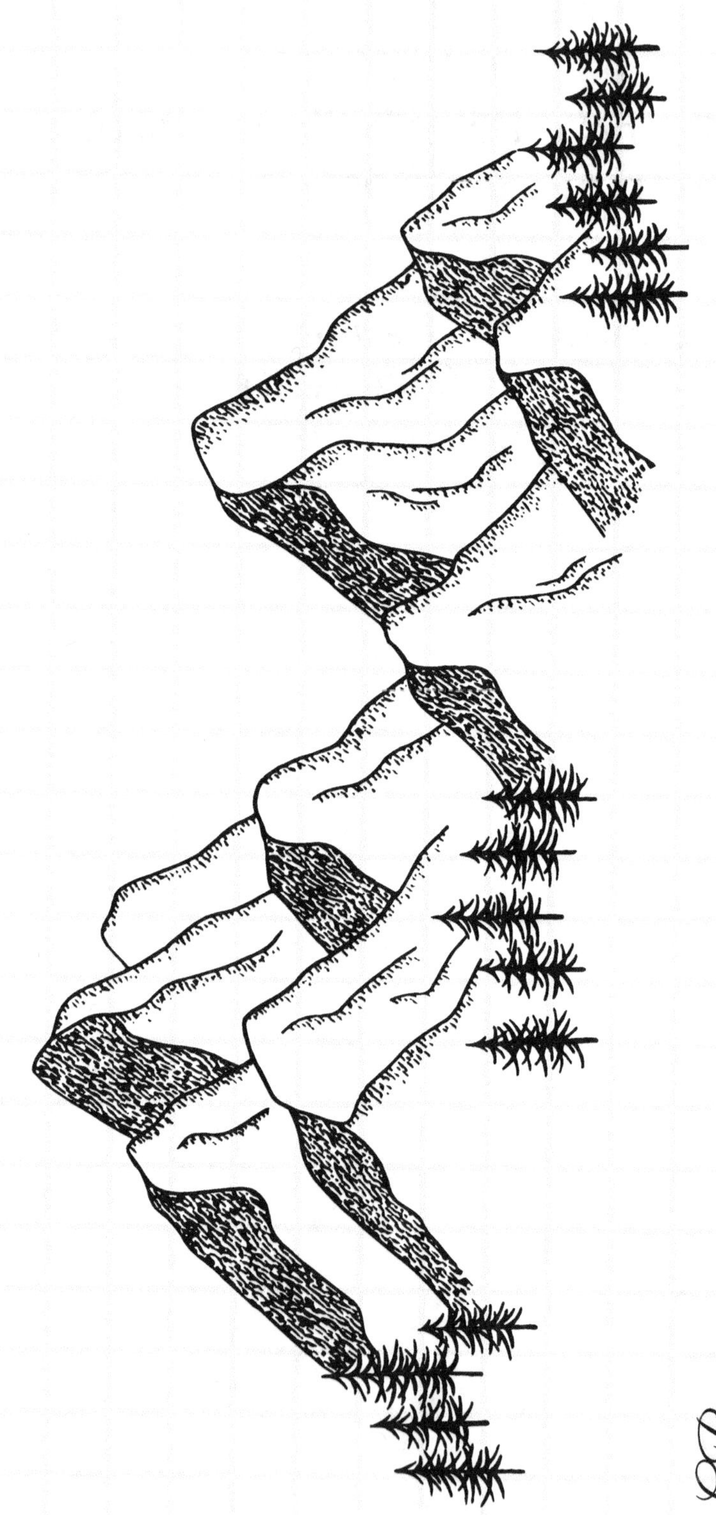

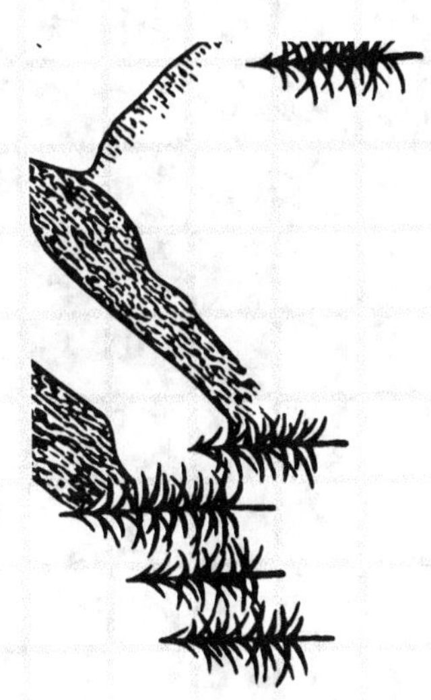

More than half of the world's fresh water originates in mountains, and all the world's major rivers are fed from mountain sources.

Good landscaping can increase the value of a house by up to 20%.

About 85% of the world's plant life is found in the ocean.

Almost 60 percent of fresh-cut flowers grown in the U.S. come from California.

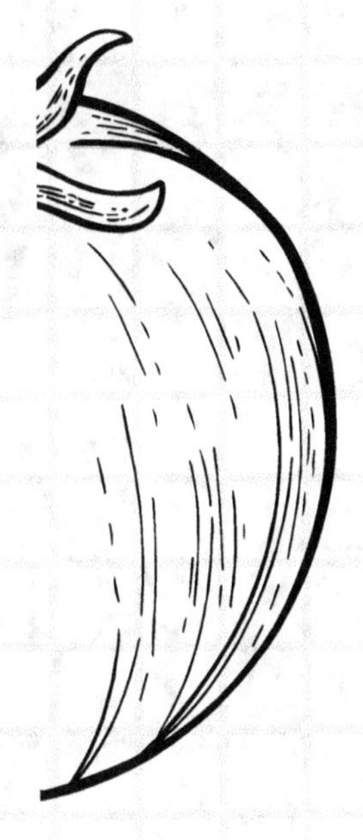

Believe it or not, tomatoes aren't always red. They can be yel-low, pink, purple, black and even white!

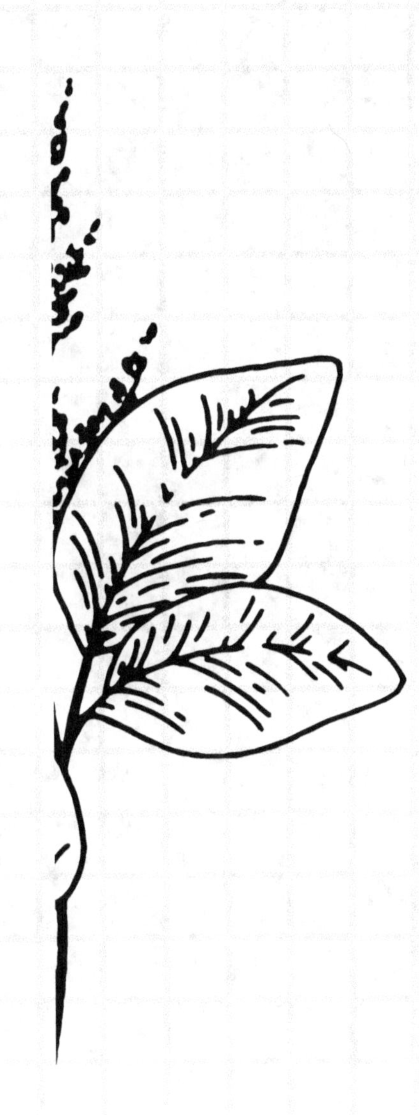

Astilbe's pyramidal feather plumes of white, pink, red, rose and purple, are surrounded by fern-like foliage so full, the flowers themselves may seem rather inconspicuous.

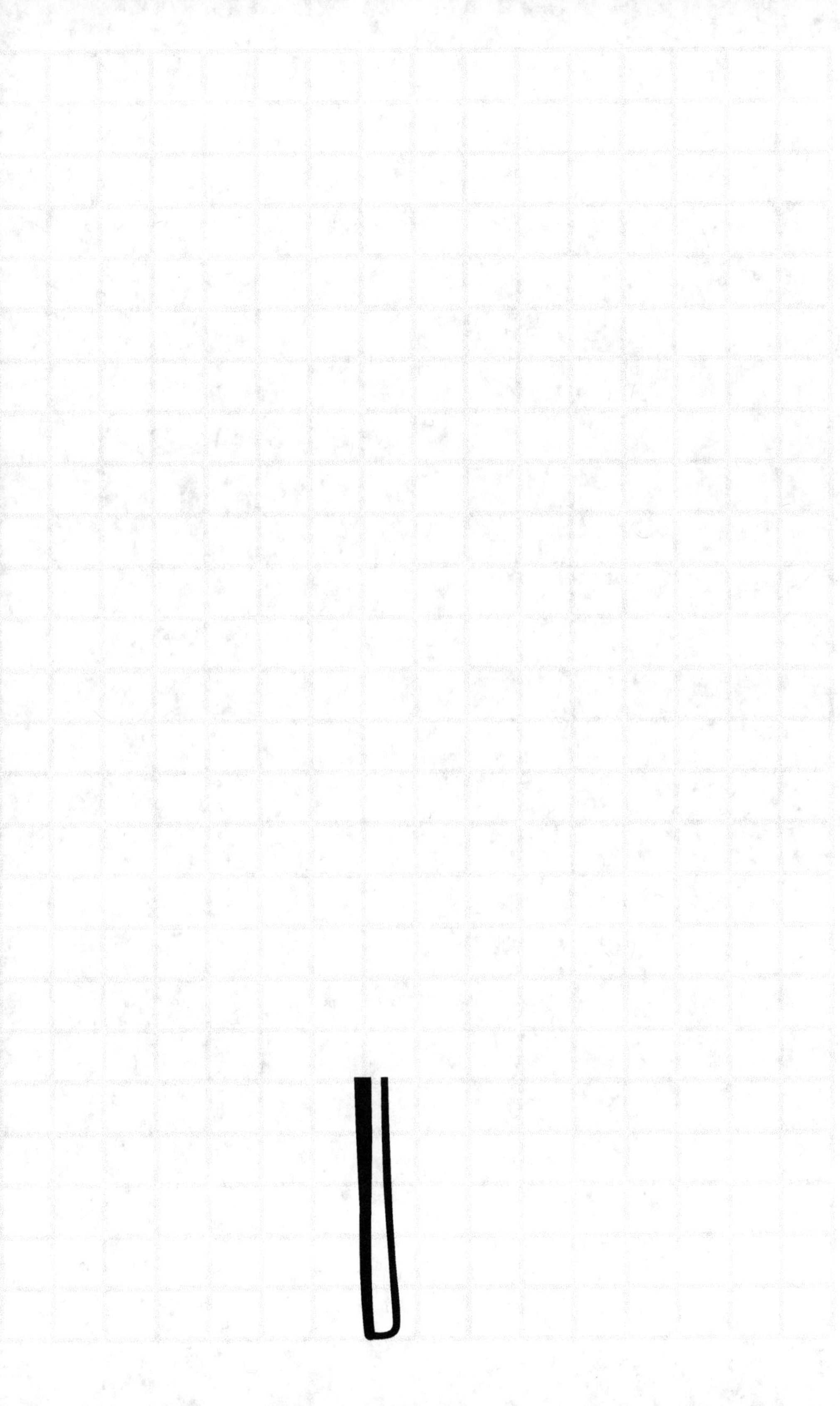

Some plants produce toxic substances that kill other plants around them-the sunflower is an example

In order to help plants to grow, fertilisers are added to the soil or sprayed on them. Manure, which is actually animal waste is a fertiliser too.

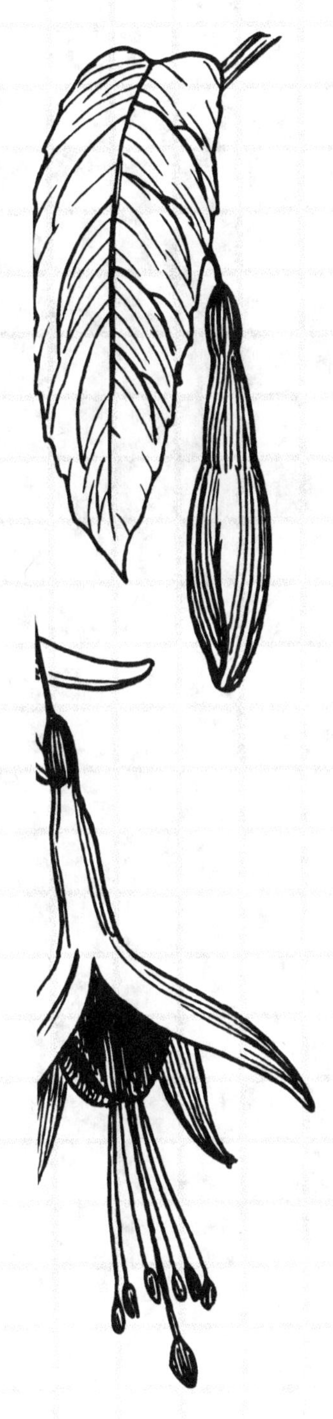

Plants convert carbon dioxide, water and minerals into food when they use energy from sunlight and this process is known as photosynthesis.

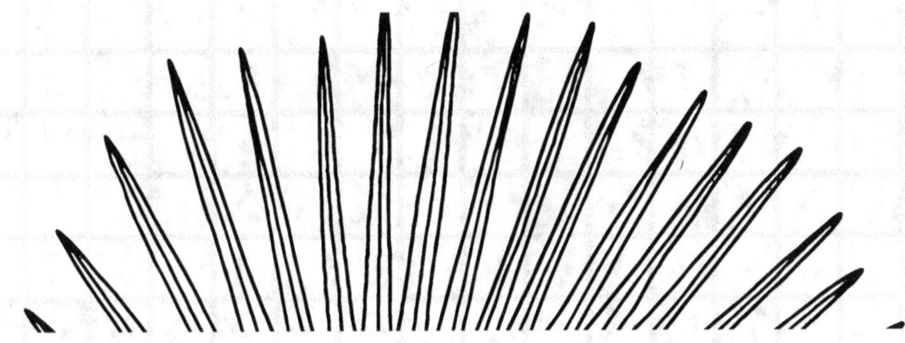

More than 20% of the world's oxygen supply is produced by the Amazon Rainforest.

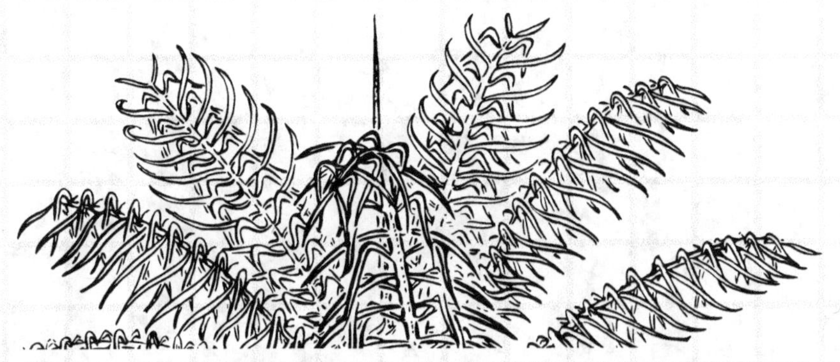

Over 2500 species of palm trees exist today

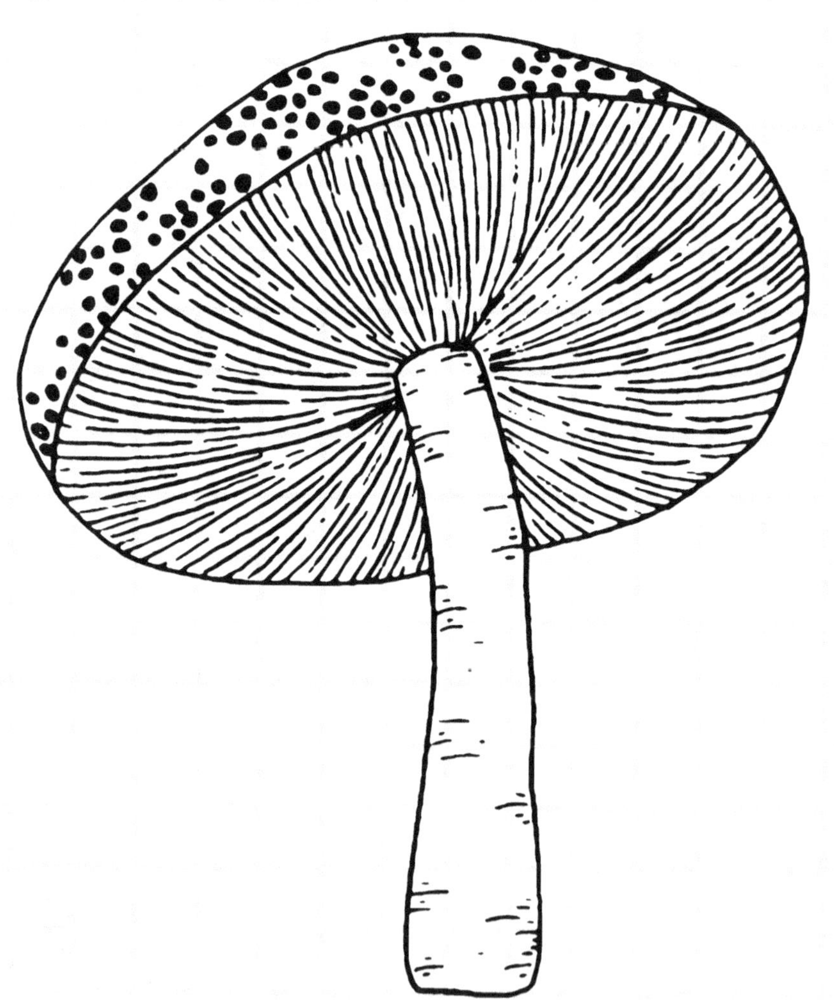

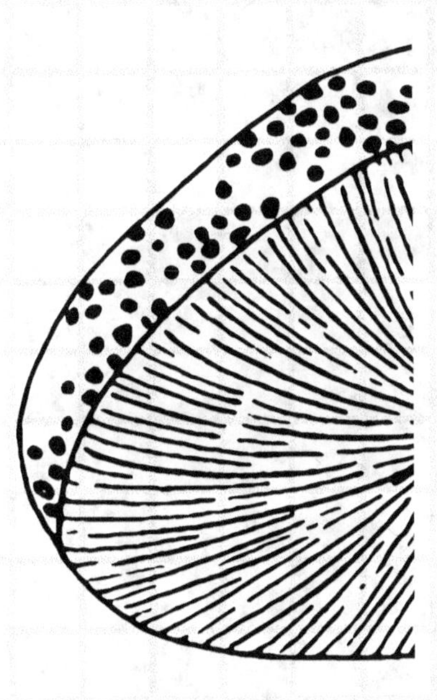

Mushrooms are a fungus, and unlike plants, mushrooms do not require sunlight to make energy for themselves.

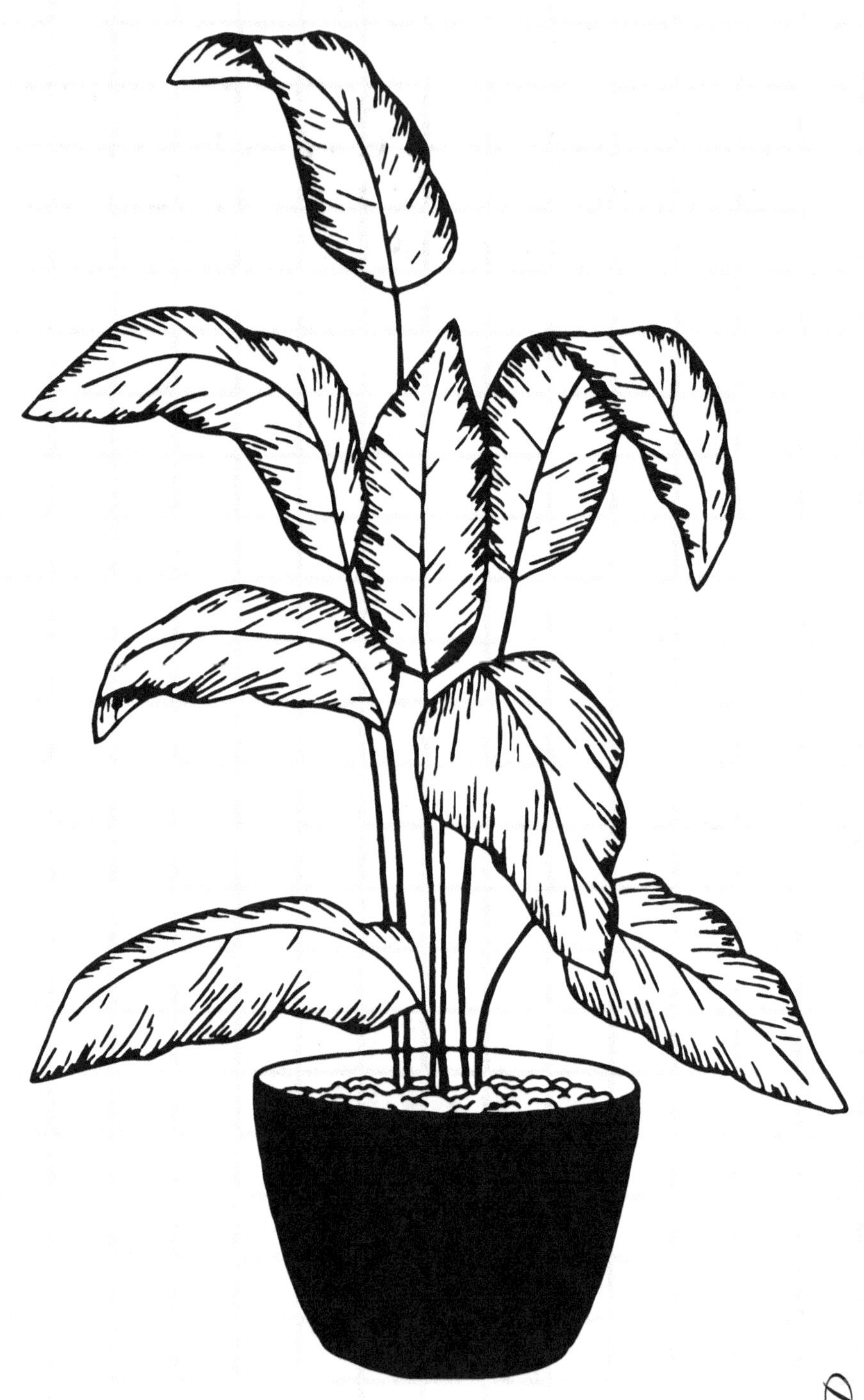

Plant roots are covered with root hairs that are used to absorb minerals and water.

Cacti life circle lasts from 15 to 300 years, depending on the species.

Trees are the longest-living organisms on earth.

Trees block noise by reducing sound waves.

Trees improve water quality

Trees help reduce the effects of climate change.

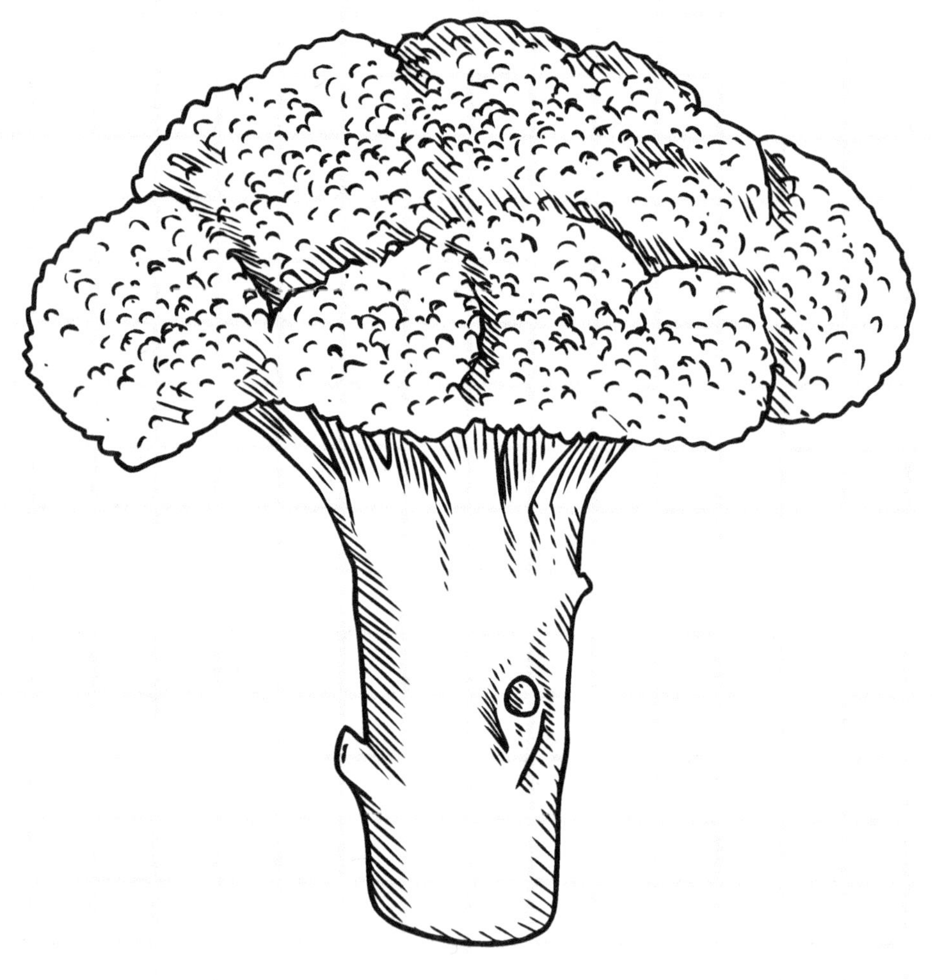

Broccoli is known as the "Crown of
Jewel Nutrition" because it is rich in
vitamins and minerals.

England's Alnwick Garden has The Poison Garden that is filled with plants which can kill you.

There are 450 species of oak trees
wordwide, but only 13 in Canada.

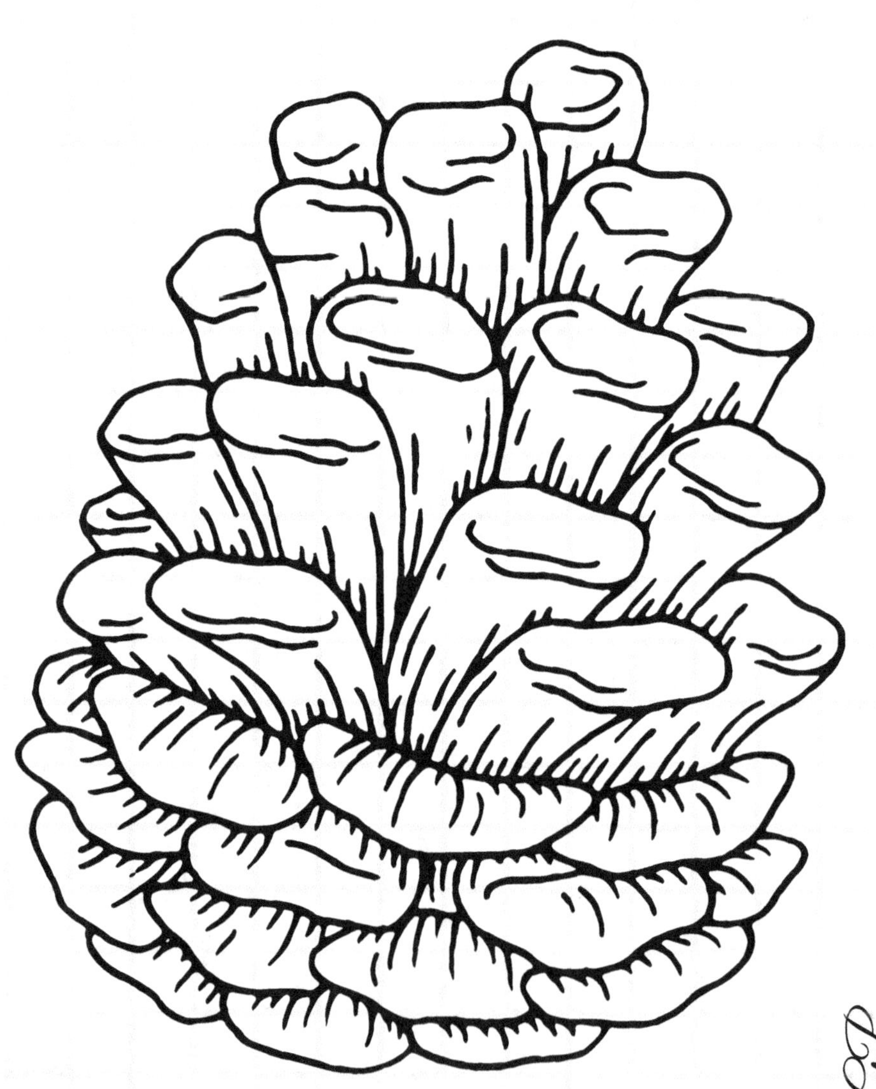

The longest pine cone measured 58.2 cm (22.9 in) on 2002 in Ohio, USA. The specimen was from a Sugar pine tree

Flowers did not always exist; they first appeared 140 million years ago.

We human beings use more than 2000 different types of plants to create various delicious food items in our meals.

SHARE YOUR DRAWINGS

Comment,rate and share the product so that I can continue to create

FB: Galas Products

Pinterest: https://pl.pinterest.com/GalasProducts

Instagram: Galasproducts

Twitter: @GalasProducts

Galas Products